Contents

DREAMWORKS
ANIMATION SKG™
Shrek is a registered trademark of DreamWorks Animation L.L.C.
Shrek the Third ™ & © 2007 DreamWorks Animation L.L.C.

Pedigree®
Published 2007
Published by Pedigree Books LTD, Beech Hill House,
Walnut Gardens, Exeter, Devon EX4 4DH
books@pedigreegroup.co.uk

£5.99

Shrek

Shrek is big, green, smelly ogre with a heart of gold. He enjoys taking mud showers and eating little forest critters. He can't wait to escape the hectic life of the kingdom and return to his simple swamp life with his wife, Fiona, and his friends Puss and Donkey. He's about to learn that marrying a princess carries a certain amount of royal responsibility.

Fiona

Princess Fiona is not your typical damsel in distress. She's smart, tough, and has been known to dropkick a band of outlaws. She also happens to be an ogre, although she is sure prettier than her husband Shrek! Having met the love of her life, Fiona has abandoned her former fairy-tale fantasies. She inspires the other princesses to do the same, helping each one to find their inner strength and break out of their pampered lifestyles.

Donkey

Donkey's got a mouth that just won't quit as well as the heart of a noble steed. Having married Dragon, Shrek's best friend is now the proud papa of a litter of dronkeys. Despite wanting to send time with his family, he is always up for an adventure and will always be at his big green friends side, whether Shrek likes it or not!

Puss In Boots

Shrek's other loyal sidekick, Puss In Boots, has the strength, bravery, and romanticism of Zorro, but in the body of a sweet little kitty-cat. Ever the Don Juan, he often gives Shrek the bachelor's point of view. Originally a hired assassin sent to dispose of Shrek by King Harold, Puss is now a valued friend to Shrek, Donkey and Fiona.

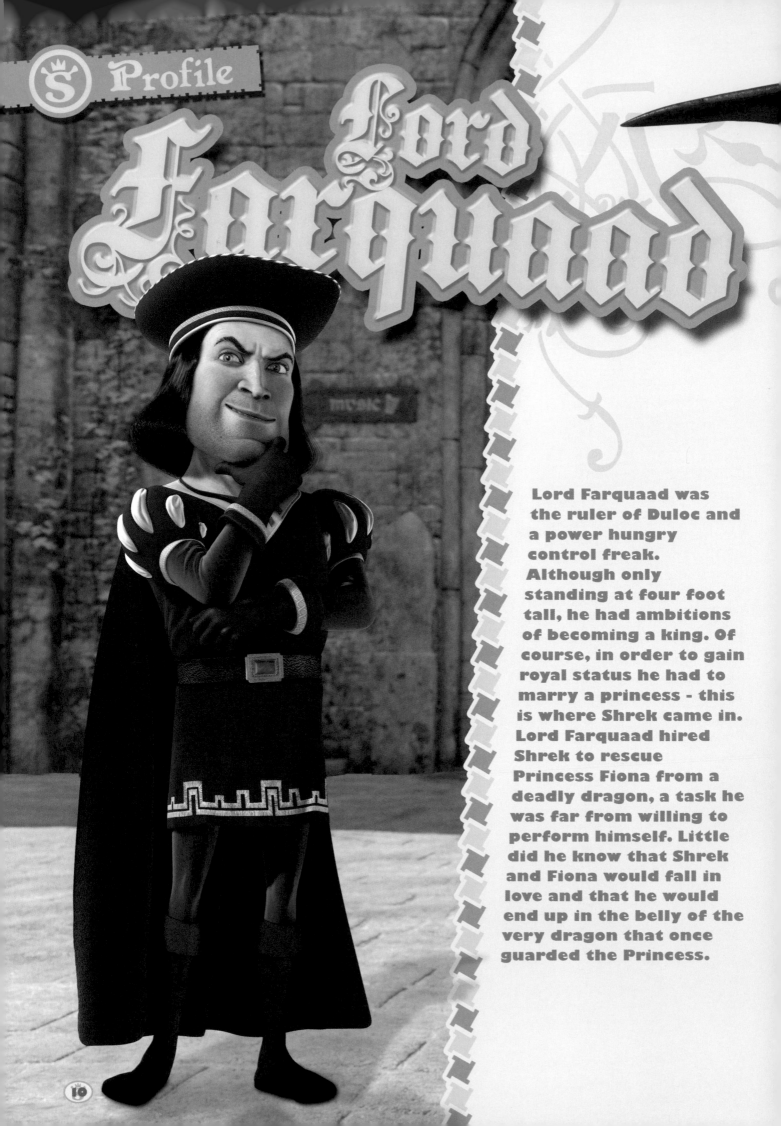

Lord Farquaad

Lord Farquaad was the ruler of Duloc and a power hungry control freak. Although only standing at four foot tall, he had ambitions of becoming a king. Of course, in order to gain royal status he had to marry a princess - this is where Shrek came in. Lord Farquaad hired Shrek to rescue Princess Fiona from a deadly dragon, a task he was far from willing to perform himself. Little did he know that Shrek and Fiona would fall in love and that he would end up in the belly of the very dragon that once guarded the Princess.

Dragon

On first impressions she may appear to be your classic fire breathing, knight-eating, village terrorising fairy-tale beast, but Dragon has a much softer side that you wouldn't expect to find in such a fearsome creature. Being trapped in the Dragon's Keep for so many years left Dragon feeling really lonely and looking for some action. So when the hapless Donkey came along, it was love at first sight!

King Harold

King Harold always tried to do what he though was best for his daughter, Fiona. When she was quite young, King Harold made a deal with Fairy Godmother to lock his daughter in a tower awaiting the kiss of Prince Charming. Even after Fiona and Shrek were married, King Harold could not accept that his daughter was hitched to an ogre and once again went into cahoots with the nasty Fairy Godmother. All of this from a guy who turned out to be a frog!

Queen Lillian

Queen Lillian is more than a typical mother. In addition to being a noble leader, she's also trained in combat. Should the Kingdom ever come under attack, the Queen really knows how to handle herself. Although she was surprised at first by her daughter's decision to marry an ogre, she soon realised that true love overcomes whatever is on the outside and that Shrek, stinky as he may be, truly loves her daughter.

Fairy Godmother

As the mother of Prince Charming, Fairy Godmother was absolutely furious when she discovered that Princess Fiona had married Shrek. You see, Fairy Godmother and King Harold had made a deal that Prince Charming would marry Princess Fiona and become next in-line to rule the Kingdom of Far Far Away. Fairy Godmother did everything she could to break up the happy couple but in the end her magic came back to bite her on the bum!

Prince Charming

Still a momma's boy at heart, Prince Charming is determined to win back his happily ever after. He's obsessed with power and fame and will not stop until he gets it. He enlists the help of the fairy-tale villains, and vows revenge upon Shrek and Fiona. Although he may look like every girls dream guy, this is one fairy-tale prince you should stay away from!

The Story So Far...

The Beginning Of A Fairy-tale

Once upon a time

there was a beautiful princess, but she was under an enchantment that could only be broken by love's first kiss.

Her father locked her away in a tall tower guarded by a terrible fire-breathing dragon. Many brave knights had tried to free her from her dreadful prison but none had prevailed. She waited in the Dragon's Keep in the highest room in the tallest tower, waiting for her true love to rescue her with love's first kiss.

Shrek awoke one morning to find that his swap had been taken over by magical creatures of the forest. The mean Lord Farquaad had exiled all of the magical critters to Shrek's swamp from all over the rest of the Kingdom.
"Who knows where this Farquaad guy is?" Shrek demanded.
"I do, me, me, pick me" Donkey shouted, jumping up and down.
"Okay," said Shrek, "You're coming with me.

16

Shrek and Donkey arrived in Duloc on Tournament Day. Turning towards the stadium, they heard Farquaad's voice, "Brave knights! You are the best and brightest in the land – and today one of you will prove himself better and brighter than the rest! That champion shall have the honour... no, the privilege, to rescue the lovely Princess Fiona from the fiery keep of the dragon! Some of you may die, but it's a sacrifice I am willing to make!"

Shrek marched straight through the row of knights, and stood defiantly in front of the podium.
"What is that?" shrieked Farquaad, looking at Shrek in horror, "It's hideous!"
"It's just a donkey!" smirked Shrek.
Farquaad considered for a second. "Knights, new plan! The one who kills the ogre will be champion!"
"Alright then. Come on!" Shrek challenged the knights. He started to work his way through them until he had floored them all. The crowd went wild.

"Thank you very much," Shrek acknowledged their cheers.
"Congratulations, ogre, you've won the honour of embarking on a great and noble quest," Farquaad announced.
Farquaad needed to marry Princess Fiona to become king. Of course he was too afraid to rescue her himself.
"Quest? I'm already on a quest," replied Shrek.
"A quest to get my swamp back! My swamp where you dumped those fairy-tale creatures."
"Alright ogre – I'll make you a deal. Go on a quest for me and I'll give you your swamp back!" Farquaad said.

And so it was settled, Shrek and Donkey would have to rescue the Princess if Shrek wanted his swamp to return to normal.

Shrek and Donkey set out on their perilous journey to rescue the Princess Fiona straight away. As they got closer and closer to the castle where she was being held, the landscape around them began to change. Soon they were surrounded by pools of lava and the stench of sulphur filled the air.

"Whew! Shrek! Did you do that? Man! You gotta warn somebody before you just crack one off like that!" cried Donkey

"Believe me, Donkey, if that was me you'd be dead," Shrek replied. "It's brimstone, we must be getting close."

They spotted the castle, set on a rock pinnacle amid a lake of molten lava. Shrek made for the rickety bridge, while Donkey peered reluctantly at the boiling lava below.
"You can't tell me you're afraid of heights," Shrek teased him. "Come on, we'll just tackle this thing together, one little baby step at a time. Just don't look down."

Donkey picked his way gingerly across the bridge,
"Shrek, I'm looking down! You gotta let me go back," he cried, as a slat fell into the lava below.
"But you're already halfway," Shrek reassured him.
"Yeah, but I know that half is safe," Donkey replied.
Suddenly Donkey realised he'd reached the other side.

"Cool!" he said with new-found confidence. "So where is this fire-breathin' pain in the neck anyway? You afraid?" whispered Donkey as they made their way through the spooky keep.

"No," Shrek replied, putting on some armour left behind by an unfortunate knight. "Now see if you can find any stairs. The Princess will be in the tallest tower. I read it in a book once."

Donkey headed off in search of a staircase,

"Cool!" he said, "You handle the dragon, I'll handle the stairs!"

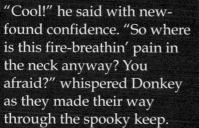

Suddenly Donkey found himself eyeball to eyeball with Dragon. He ran in the opposite direction, a fireball close behind him. As Dragon closed in on Donkey, Shrek grabbed her tail. She whipped her tail around, sending him hurtling into the air and clean through the wall of the princess's bedchamber. Now Donkey was trapped by Dragon.
"Why what large teeth you have...," he stuttered, "I mean white, sparkling teeth. I know you probably hear this all the time... from your food... but you must bleach or something, 'cause that is one dazzling smile you've got there."

Donkey stumbled on as Dragon smiled sweetly "You know what else? You're, you're a girl dragon. I mean, you're just reeking of feminine beauty! Hey, I'd just love to stick around, but I'm an asthmatic and I don't know if it'll work out, what with you blowing those smoke rings and stuff," Donkey coughed. "Shrek! Help! Shreeeekkk!"

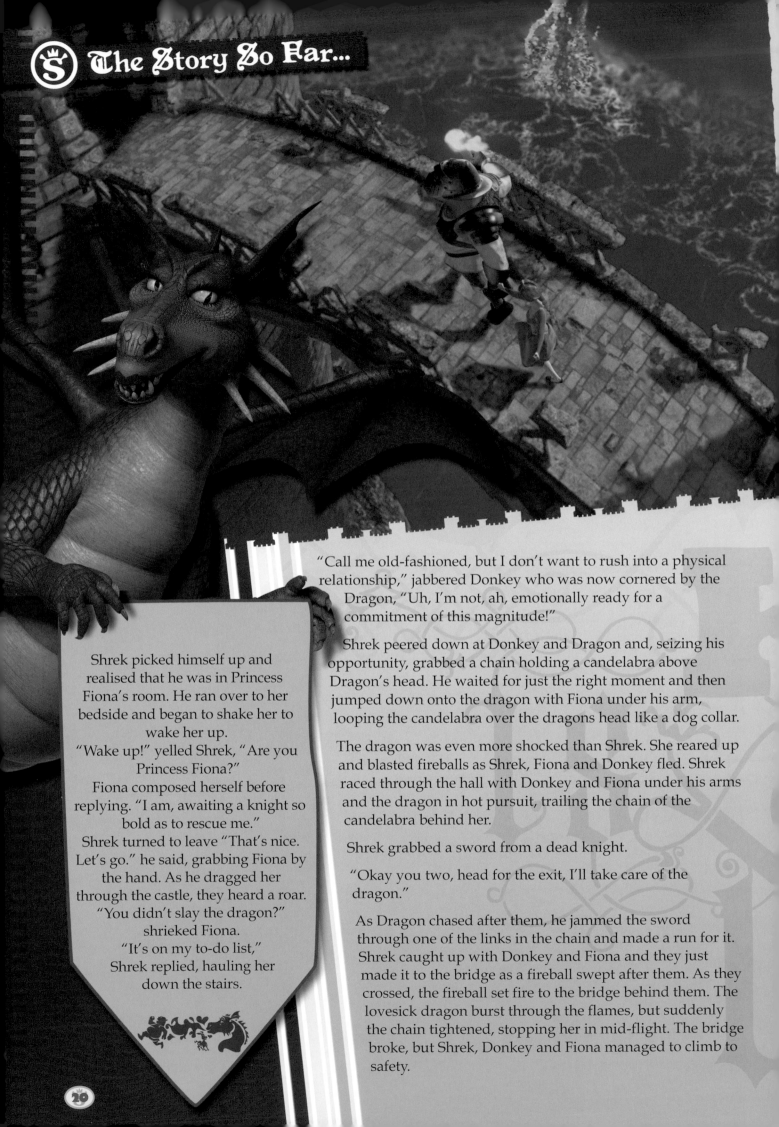

"Call me old-fashioned, but I don't want to rush into a physical relationship," jabbered Donkey who was now cornered by the Dragon, "Uh, I'm not, ah, emotionally ready for a commitment of this magnitude!"

Shrek peered down at Donkey and Dragon and, seizing his opportunity, grabbed a chain holding a candelabra above Dragon's head. He waited for just the right moment and then jumped down onto the dragon with Fiona under his arm, looping the candelabra over the dragons head like a dog collar.

The dragon was even more shocked than Shrek. She reared up and blasted fireballs as Shrek, Fiona and Donkey fled. Shrek raced through the hall with Donkey and Fiona under his arms and the dragon in hot pursuit, trailing the chain of the candelabra behind her.

Shrek grabbed a sword from a dead knight.

"Okay you two, head for the exit, I'll take care of the dragon."

As Dragon chased after them, he jammed the sword through one of the links in the chain and made a run for it. Shrek caught up with Donkey and Fiona and they just made it to the bridge as a fireball swept after them. As they crossed, the fireball set fire to the bridge behind them. The lovesick dragon burst through the flames, but suddenly the chain tightened, stopping her in mid-flight. The bridge broke, but Shrek, Donkey and Fiona managed to climb to safety.

Shrek picked himself up and realised that he was in Princess Fiona's room. He ran over to her bedside and began to shake her to wake her up.
"Wake up!" yelled Shrek, "Are you Princess Fiona?"
Fiona composed herself before replying. "I am, awaiting a knight so bold as to rescue me."
Shrek turned to leave "That's nice. Let's go." he said, grabbing Fiona by the hand. As he dragged her through the castle, they heard a roar.
"You didn't slay the dragon?" shrieked Fiona.
"It's on my to-do list," Shrek replied, hauling her down the stairs.

"You did it! You rescued me! You're amazing, you're wonderful, you're... a little unorthodox, I'll admit, but... thy deed is great and thine heart is pure. I am eternally in your debt!" gushed Fiona. "The battle is won," she continued. "You may remove your helmet, good sir knight."

Shrek stalled for a minute, "Ahhh... no. I... I have helmet hair."

"Now remove your helmet!" Fiona ordered.

"Okay! Easy. As you command, Your Highness..." he added, removing the helmet.

"You're... an ogre?!" Fiona stuttered, staring at him blankly.

"Oh, you were expecting Prince Charming?" asked Shrek, giving her a long-suffering look. "Princess, I was sent to rescue you by Lord Farquaad, okay? He's the one who wants to marry you."

"Well, I'm sorry. You can tell Lord Farquaad that if he wants to rescue me properly I'll be waiting for him right here!" Fiona told him, determined not to move.

Throwing Fiona over his shoulder, Shrek set off.

"You coming, Donkey?" he called. Suddenly Fiona found herself dumped unceremoniously on the ground.

"Shouldn't we stop to make camp?" she said nervously, looking at the setting sun, "There are robbers in the woods."

"Hey, come on, I'm scarier than anything we're gonna see in this forest," Shrek interrupted sarcastically.

"I NEED SOMEWHERE TO CAMP NOW!" Fiona yelled at him.

"Okay, over here!" Shrek called, rolling a boulder from the mouth of a cave.

"It's perfect!" said Fiona, ripping some bark off a nearby tree to make a door.

"Well, Gentlemen, I bid thee goodnight."

"Hey Shrek... What we going to do when we get our swamp back?" asked Donkey as they gazed at the stars.

"There's no we, " Shrek replied. "There's just me and my swamp. And the first thing I am going to do is build a ten-foot wall around my land."

"You cut me deep, Shrek, you cut me real deep..." said Donkey. "You know, I think this whole 'wall' thing is just a way to keep somebody out. What's your problem? What you got against the whole world?"

"Look I'm not the one with the problem, okay? It's the whole world that seems to have a problem with me." Shrek sighed. "People take one look at me and go, 'Aaagh! Help! Run! A big, stupid, ugly ogre!' That's why I'm better off alone."

The next morning the trio awoke and continued on their journey back to Duloc. As they walked through the forest, Robin Hood jumped down from a tree and grabbed Princess Fiona.

"I am your saviour and I am rescuing you from this green beast," he said, kissing her hand.

Fiona kicked Robin into the air and he landed against a rock, knocked out cold. Then, while arrows flew around her, Fiona did a back flip and took out the Merry Men, one by one, with a series of martial arts moves.

"Whoa, where did that come from?" asked Shrek, impressed.

"Well when one lives alone one has to learn these things," Fiona laughed nervously, "Hey, there's an arrow in your butt!"

Donkey started to panic, "Shrek's gonna die. You can't do this to me Shrek! Keep your legs elevated. Turn yer head and cough. Does anyone know the Heimlich?"

Fiona decided to get rid of Donkey, and told him to go and look for a blue flower with red thorns.

"Blue flower, red thorns." Donkey repeated to himself as he searched in the forest.

"OK I'm on it! Don't die Shrek. And if you see a long tunnel, STAY AWAY FROM THE LIGHT!"

Meanwhile, Fiona ripped the arrow from his butt. "Ooww!"

"Is that blood?" asked Donkey, passing out. Shrek picked him up and they continued on their way.

By late afternoon they had left the woods and Duloc stretched out before them.

"There it is," said Shrek "I guess we better move on."

Fiona gave Shrek a meaningful glance, "But Shrek, I'm worried about Donkey. He doesn't look so good."

Shrek suddenly caught on, "She's right. You look awful," he told Donkey, "Who's hungry? I'll find us some dinner."

"Mmm. Mmm. This is really good! What is this?" asked Fiona, when she tasted the food that Shrek had cooked.

"Weedrat. Rôtisserie-style," Shrek informed her proudly. "They're also great in stews – I make a mean weedrat stew. Maybe you can come and visit me in the swamp sometime. Um, Princess?" Shrek continued nervously.

"Yes... Shrek?" Fiona replied expectantly.

"I, um, I was wondering, are you... are you gonna eat that?" asked Shrek, pointing at the last weedrat.

"Man," Donkey piped up, "Isn't this romantic, just look at that sunset."

Fiona leapt to her feet, a desperate look on her face.

"Sunset!! Oh no! I mean... it's late. I'd better go inside," she cried, heading for an old mill.

onkey followed Princess Fiona into the barn to check that she was alright.

"Princess, where are you? It's very spooky in here…" he called out into the darkness. Suddenly from out of the shadows stepped a very large, green ogress.

"Ahhhh!" shrieked Donkey.

"Ahhhh!" shrieked the ogress.

"What'd you do with the Princess?" Donkey demanded.

"Shhhhhh! I'm the Princess. It's me. In this body," the ogress replied in Fiona's voice. "Oh my God. You ate the Princess!!! Can you hear me?!" shouted Donkey at the ogress's stomach.

"Shhh! I've been this way as long as I can remember. It only happens when the sun goes down. By night one way, by day another. This shall be the norm.

Until you find true love's first kiss. And then take love's true form. That's why I have to marry Lord Farquaad tomorrow before the sun sets and he sees me… like this."

"Princess, how about if you don't marry Farquaad? You know, you're kind of an ogre and Shrek - well, you've got a lot in common," Donkey suggested.

"Take a good look at me, Donkey. I mean really…"

Shrek stopped at the door of the mill with a flower for Fiona and overheard the Princess talking to Donkey

"…who could ever love a beast so hideous and ugly? And princess and ugly don't go together. That's why I can't stay here with Shrek. I have to marry my true love. It's the only way to break the spell."

Stunned and hurt, Shrek dropped the flower and walked away. Fiona made Donkey promise not to tell anyone her secret. When he left, Fiona found the flower and lay awake, picking off the petals one by one. "I tell him, I tell him not, I tell him," she chanted and eventually came to a decision.

She headed for the door in search of Shrek. As the ogress stepped outside, the sun rose, and she turned back into a beautiful princess.

"Shrek! There's something I have to tell you."

She stopped, noticing that Shrek looked mighty mad.

"You don't have to tell me anything." he said, "I heard enough last night - 'Who could love such a hideous and ugly beast?'"

"I thought that wouldn't matter to you," Fiona said.

"Well it does," Shrek told her. Shrek had misunderstood what he had overheard Fiona and Donley talking about. He thought that Fiona had been calling him hideous and ugly!

The Story So Far...

Before Princess Fiona could explain they were interrupted by the approach of Lord Farquaad and his army.

"Here's the deed to your swamp, ogre, cleared out as agreed. Take it and go, before I change my mind! Forgive me, Princess, for startling you," Farquaad continued, "But I have never seen such a radiant beauty before."

He took Fiona's hand, "Princess Fiona, I ask your hand in marriage."

"I accept," she replied, glaring at Shrek.

"Excellent! I'll start the plans, for tomorrow we wed!" Farquaad declared.

"No, let's get married today, before sunset." Fiona blurted out.

"Oh, anxious are we?" asked Farquaad. "You're right, the sooner the better. Captain, round up some guests!"

As they left for Duloc, Fiona turned to Shrek, "Fare thee well, ogre." she said spitefully.

Sadly Shrek returned to his swamp and sat down to dinner, but he had no appetite. Suddenly he heard a noise outside and went to investigate.

"Donkey! What are you doing?" he shouted.

"You of all people should recognise a wall when you see one!" Donkey replied.

"Well – yeah," said Shrek, "But it's supposed to go around my swamp, not through it."

"It is. Around your half. That's your half and this is my half. I helped rescue the princess and I get half the booty" Donkey explained.

"This is my swamp!" Shrek exploded.

"With you it's always me, me, me. You are mean to me, you insult me and you don't appreciate anything that I do," Donkey complained.

"Oh yeah – well if I treated you so bad how come you came back?" Shrek demanded. "There you are doing it again. Just like you did to Fiona.

And all she ever did was like you. Maybe even love you," Donkey continued.

"Love me?" asked Shrek, astonished, "She said I was ugly! A hideous creature!"

"She wasn't talking about you!" Donkey explained.

"She wasn't talking about me? Well, what DID she say about me then?" Shrek asked.

"Why don't you ask her yourself?" Donkey replied.

"The wedding!" Shrek shouted with a start. "We'll never make it in time!"

"Never fear. Where there's a will there's a way... and I have a way," said Donkey.

To Shrek's surprise, Dragon flew in. They climbed on her back and she flew them to the cathedral in Duloc.

》》》

Meanwhile, at the castle in Duloc the wedding ceremony had already started and the Bishop was welcoming the guests.

"People of Duloc, we gather here today to bear witness to the union of our new King and Queen."

Fiona glanced nervously at the window, where the sun was going down, and interrupted the Bishop.

"Um... Excuse me... ah... Could we just skip ahead to the 'I dos'?"

Farquaad was about to kiss his new bride, when Shrek burst into the cathedral.

"I object!" he yelled. "Fiona, you can't marry him! He's just marrying you so he can be King. He's not your true love!"

Farquaad puckered his lips, "Fiona, my love, we're but a kiss away from our happily-ever-after," he said.

Fiona backed away and turned to Shrek. "By night one way, by day another..." she said. "I wanted to show you before..." .

As the sun set, she closed her eyes and waited. As Fiona transformed, Farquaad's eyes grew wide with shock and revulsion. But Shrek smiled.

"Ahhh... that explains a lot!" he said.

"Guards!! I order you to get them out of my sight!" Farquaad shouted, grabbing the crown from the podium. "All this hocus pocus alters nothing. This marriage is binding and that makes me King! Insolent beasts, I'll make you regret the day we met!" Farquaad yelled, as the guards dragged Shrek away.

"And as for you, my wife! I'll have you locked back in that tower for the rest of your days!!!"

Suddenly the window shattered and Dragon's head appeared.

"Alright," shouted Donkey, sitting astride Dragon, "Nobody move. I got a dragon here and I'm not afraid to use it! I'm a donkey on the edge!"

And then Dragon swallowed Farquaad in one gulp.

"I love you," said Shrek, turning to Fiona.

"I love you too," she replied.

As they kissed, a magical glow surrounded Fiona and she floated up towards the ceiling,

then fell back to the ground. She was still an ogress.

"I don't understand," she said, "I'm supposed to be beautiful."

"But you are beautiful," Shrek told her.

Shrek and Fiona were married in the swamp and all the fairy-tale creatures and Dulocians joined in the celebrations. When Fiona threw her bouquet, it was caught by Dragon, who turned to Donkey batting her eyelids.

The End
...FOR NOW!

29

Spot The Difference

In the two pictures below there are eight small differences. Can you spot them? Shrek, Fiona, Puss and Donkey have made it really difficult for you so try your best to complete this quest!

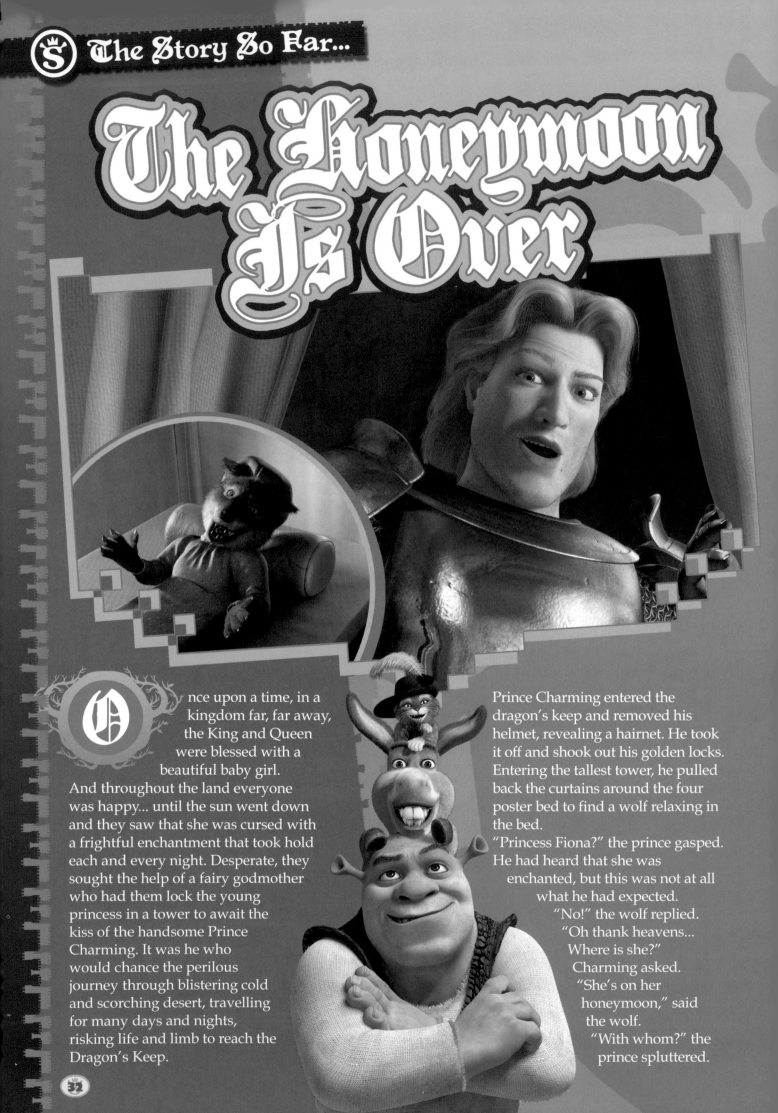

The Honeymoon Is Over

Once upon a time, in a kingdom far, far away, the King and Queen were blessed with a beautiful baby girl. And throughout the land everyone was happy... until the sun went down and they saw that she was cursed with a frightful enchantment that took hold each and every night. Desperate, they sought the help of a fairy godmother who had them lock the young princess in a tower to await the kiss of the handsome Prince Charming. It was he who would chance the perilous journey through blistering cold and scorching desert, travelling for many days and nights, risking life and limb to reach the Dragon's Keep.

Prince Charming entered the dragon's keep and removed his helmet, revealing a hairnet. He took it off and shook out his golden locks. Entering the tallest tower, he pulled back the curtains around the four poster bed to find a wolf relaxing in the bed.

"Princess Fiona?" the prince gasped. He had heard that she was enchanted, but this was not at all what he had expected.

"No!" the wolf replied.

"Oh thank heavens... Where is she?" Charming asked.

"She's on her honeymoon," said the wolf.

"With whom?" the prince spluttered.

Meanwhile Shrek and Fiona were on their way back to Shrek's swamp after enjoying their honeymoon at Hansel's Honeymoon Hideaway.
"It's so good to be home, just you and me," Shrek sighed, as he and Fiona returned to the swamp.
Opening the door he found Donkey sitting in his favourite chair.
"Donkey, shouldn't you be getting home to Dragon?" Fiona asked hopefully.
"Dragon's been all moody lately, so I thought I'd move back in with you guys," Donkey said, with what he hoped was a winning smile.
"But, Donkey, Fiona and I are married now. We need time together ALONE," Shrek tried to explain.

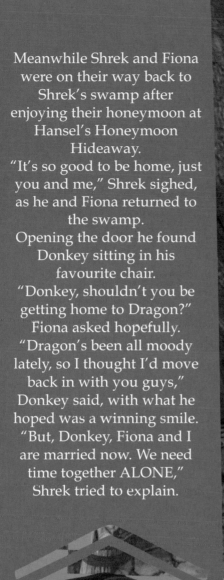

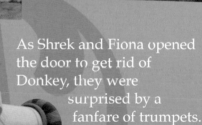

As Shrek and Fiona opened the door to get rid of Donkey, they were surprised by a fanfare of trumpets.
"Dearest Princess Fiona," read a page, "You are hereby summoned to the Kingdom of Far Far Away for a royal ball in celebration of your marriage at which time the King will bestow his royal blessing upon you and your Prince Charming. Love, the King and Queen of Far Far Away, aka Mum and Dad."
"We are not going!" Shrek declared. "Trust me, it's a bad idea. That's final!"

≫

he following morning Shrek reluctantly loaded suitcases onto the onion carriage. Donkey jumped on top of the luggage. "Hey, c'mon, Shrek, we don't want to hit traffic," he said.

The fairy-tale creatures waved goodbye then ran into Shrek's house to party.

"Are we there yet?" asked Donkey as they passed a sign reading '700 miles to Far Away'.

"Are we there yet?" asked Donkey as they drove through the mountains past a sign reading '200 miles to Away'.

"Are we there yet?" asked Donkey as they travelled through a forest past a sign reading '100 miles to Far Far Away'.

"NO WE ARE NOT!" Shrek yelled.

"This is taking forever," Donkey moaned, "There ain't no inflight movie or nothing."

Shrek gritted his teeth, "The Kingdom of Far Far Away, Donkey, that's where we're going... FAR... FAR... AWAY!!"

Finally, the carriage entered the city. Shrek and Fiona smiled nervously at each other as they pulled up outside the castle. Crowds clapped and cheered either side of the red carpet, while the King and Queen waited expectantly at the entrance.

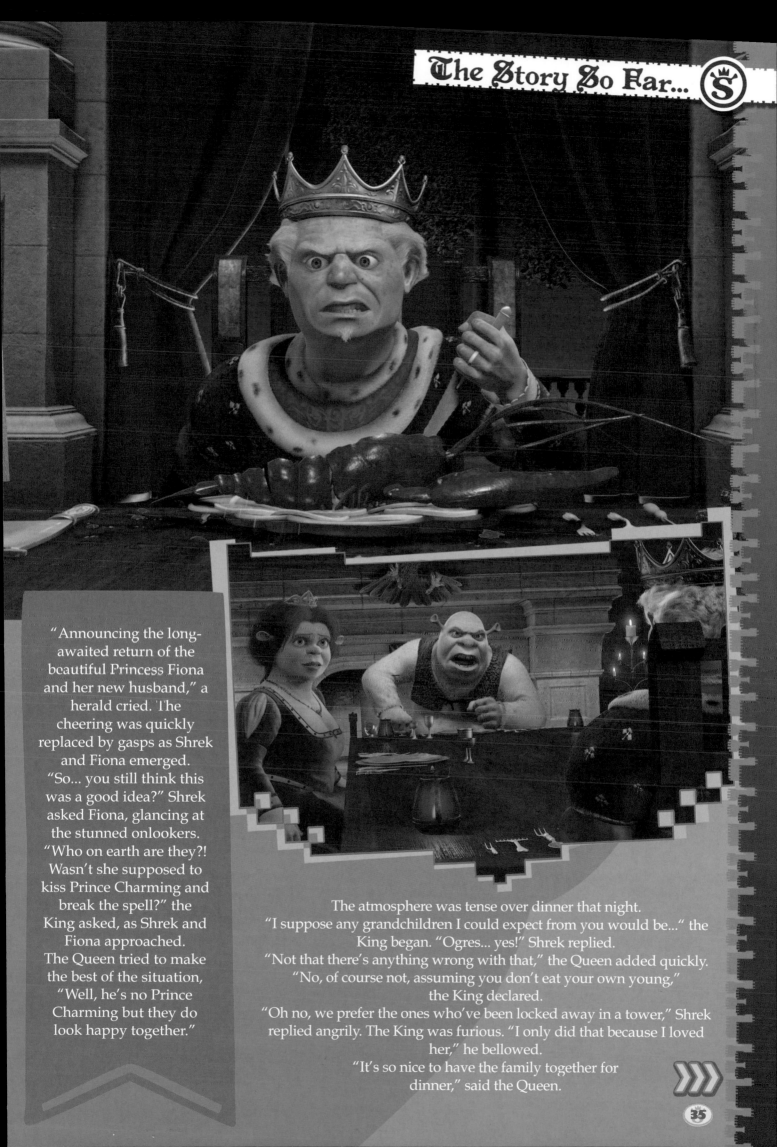

"Announcing the long-awaited return of the beautiful Princess Fiona and her new husband," a herald cried. The cheering was quickly replaced by gasps as Shrek and Fiona emerged. "So... you still think this was a good idea?" Shrek asked Fiona, glancing at the stunned onlookers. "Who on earth are they?! Wasn't she supposed to kiss Prince Charming and break the spell?" the King asked, as Shrek and Fiona approached. The Queen tried to make the best of the situation, "Well, he's no Prince Charming but they do look happy together."

The atmosphere was tense over dinner that night. "I suppose any grandchildren I could expect from you would be..." the King began. "Ogres... yes!" Shrek replied. "Not that there's anything wrong with that," the Queen added quickly. "No, of course not, assuming you don't eat your own young," the King declared. "Oh no, we prefer the ones who've been locked away in a tower," Shrek replied angrily. The King was furious. "I only did that because I loved her," he bellowed. "It's so nice to have the family together for dinner," said the Queen.

Fiona was so upset about the dinner argument that she ran from the dining table and up to her bedroom. She stepped out onto her balcony and a tear drop rolled down her face onto the railing. Suddenly a huge bubble appeared. Inside it was Fairy Godmother.

"Ahhh!!!" cried Fairy Godmother when she saw that Fiona was an ogress. "I'm your Fairy Godmother," she explained. "With just a wave of my magic wand your troubles will be gone, With a flick of the wrist and just a flash, you'll land a prince with a ton of cash." Enchanted pieces of furniture started to dance around the room, surrounding Fiona. They were interrupted by a knock at the door as Shrek and Donkey burst in. "Ah... Fairy Godmother, furniture... I'd like you to meet my husband, Shrek," Fairy Godmother stared in shock. "Your husband? When did this happen? That can't be right!" She turned to leave, then offered her card to Fiona. "Remember, if you ever need me... Happiness... It's just a teardrop away." Shrek grabbed the card, "Thanks, but we have all the happiness we need!"

we all have our pretty side

EVERY THING is always about YOU

The
GREEN DUDE
with the
Bad Attitude

OGRES ROCK

"Fiona was supposed to choose the prince we picked out for her. Instead our daughter has married a monster," the King moaned to his wife that night, as he paced up and down in front of the bedroom window. Suddenly Fairy Godmother's carriage appeared outside. The King rushed out onto the balcony, quickly closing the shutters behind him.

"Get in!" Fairy Godmother ordered. Sitting beside her was Prince Charming. "We need to talk. You remember my son? He endures blistering winds and scorching desert! He climbs to the highest room of the tallest tower... and what does he find? Some wolf telling him that HIS princess is already married! We made a deal, Harold, and I assume you don't want me to go back on my part! So Fiona and Charming WILL be together. It's what's best... not only for your daughter but for your kingdom!" The king was shoved back out onto his balcony and the carriage zoomed off.

Later that night the King wrapped himself in a cloak and rode to The Poison Apple. He went into the gloomy bar and whispered to the ugly stepsister behind the counter, "I need to have someone taken care of. He's an ogre." She directed him to a room at the back. A pair of eyes glinted in the darkness. "I'm told you're the one to talk to about an ogre problem," the King said hesitantly, handing over a large sack of gold.

nable to sleep, Shrek wandered around Fiona's bedroom. He flicked open young Fiona's diary and read, 'Dad says I'm going away for a while. And Mum says, when I'm old enough, my handsome Prince Charming will rescue me and bring me back to my family.'
Hearing someone outside, Shrek opened the bedroom door and was surprised to see King Harold.
"I wanted to apologise for my despicable behaviour," he told Shrek. "Would you join me for a morning hunt? A little father-son time. Shall we say 7:30 by the old oak?"

Next morning Shrek and Donkey were looking for the old oak tree when they heard a purring sound. Suddenly a cat armed with a sword jumped out from behind a tree.
"Ha ha! Fear me... if you DARE!!!" it hissed.
"It's a cat," Shrek said playfully, "C'mere little kitty, kitty, kitty."
Puss In Boots leapt out of his boots and dug his claws into Shrek's thigh. He disappeared inside the ogre's shirt, then ripped his way out. Shrek grabbed the cat by the scruff of his neck.
"Please, it was nothing personal, Señor," Puss pleaded, "I was doing it for my family. The King offered me much in gold and I have a litter of brothers."

"Whoah, whoah, Fiona's father paid you to do this?" asked Shrek dismayed. "Oh come on Shrek," said Donkey trying to comfort him, "Almost everybody that meets you wants to kill you."

Shrek stared at his reflection in the stream. "Maybe Fiona would have been better off if I were some sort of Prince Charming," he said sadly. "I just wish I could make her happy." Suddenly he remembered something. He took a card from his pocket. 'Happiness... A teardrop away,' he read. "Donkey, think of the saddest thing that's ever happened to you."

"Well, there was the time that old farmer tried to sell me for some magic beans. Then this fool had a party and all the guests tried to pin the tail on me. Then they tried to beat me with a stick shouting 'piñata'..." Donkey began.
"No, Donkey, I need you to cry," said Shrek.
Suddenly Puss stepped on Donkey's hoof with the heel of his boot.
"UUGGGGHHHH," Donkey yelled, a tear coming to his eye.
Shrek quickly held the card under it. The teardrop turned into a bubble and from inside came the voice of Fairy Godmother, "I'm either away from my desk or with a client, but if you come by the office we'll be glad to make you a personal appointment. Have a happy ever after."

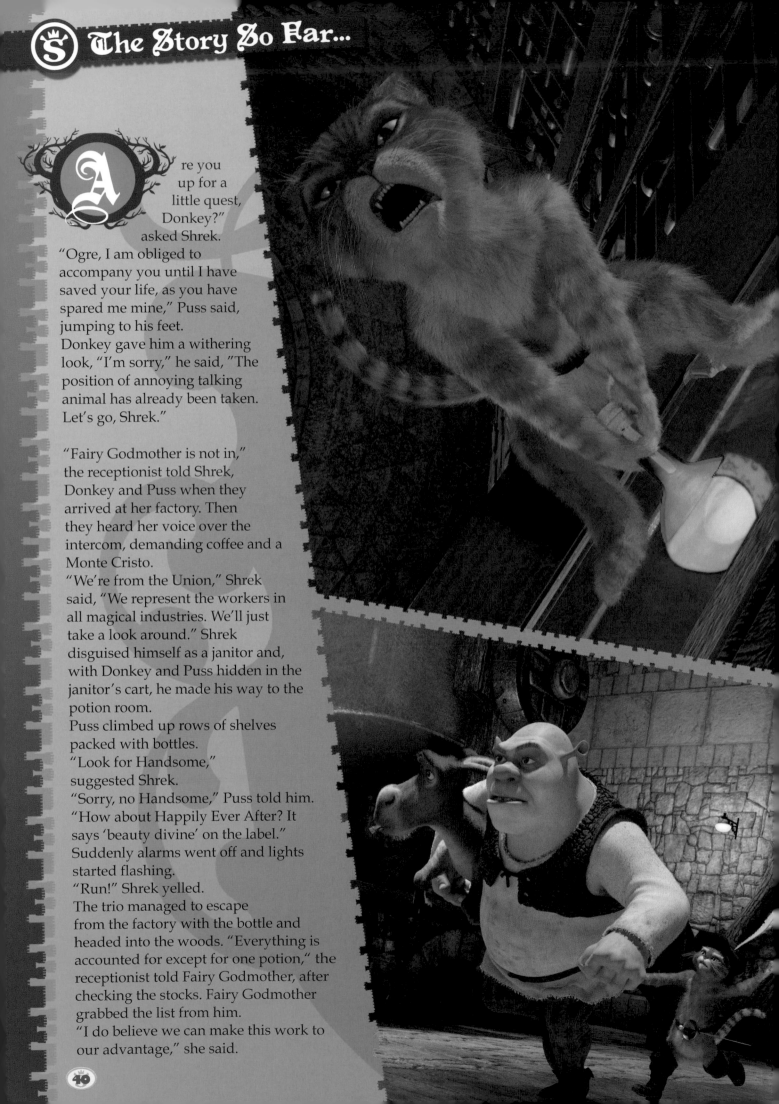

"Are you up for a little quest, Donkey?" asked Shrek.

"Ogre, I am obliged to accompany you until I have saved your life, as you have spared me mine," Puss said, jumping to his feet.

Donkey gave him a withering look, "I'm sorry," he said, "The position of annoying talking animal has already been taken. Let's go, Shrek."

"Fairy Godmother is not in," the receptionist told Shrek, Donkey and Puss when they arrived at her factory. Then they heard her voice over the intercom, demanding coffee and a Monte Cristo.

"We're from the Union," Shrek said, "We represent the workers in all magical industries. We'll just take a look around." Shrek disguised himself as a janitor and, with Donkey and Puss hidden in the janitor's cart, he made his way to the potion room.

Puss climbed up rows of shelves packed with bottles.

"Look for Handsome," suggested Shrek.

"Sorry, no Handsome," Puss told him. "How about Happily Ever After? It says 'beauty divine' on the label."

Suddenly alarms went off and lights started flashing.

"Run!" Shrek yelled.

The trio managed to escape from the factory with the bottle and headed into the woods. "Everything is accounted for except for one potion," the receptionist told Fairy Godmother, after checking the stocks. Fairy Godmother grabbed the list from him.

"I do believe we can make this work to our advantage," she said.

"If one of you drinks this, you both will be fine," Shrek read from the label on the bottle. "I guess it means it will affect Fiona too."

"Boss, in case there is something wrong with the potion allow me to take the first sip," offered Puss.

Donkey snatched the bottle, "If there's going to be any animal testing, I'm going to do it," he said, taking a swig.

They waited expectantly but nothing happened.

"Maybe it doesn't work on donkeys," said Shrek, downing the potion.

Storm clouds gathered as they ran to a disused barn to shelter from the rain. Donkey started to feel dizzy and promptly passed out. Then Shrek got woozy and crashed to the ground. A puff of magical blue smoke burst through the door and windows of the barn. At the same moment, blue smoke burst from Fiona's window back at the castle.

When Shrek woke up the following morning, he was surrounded by three pretty young women.

"Oww. My head...," he groaned.

"Here, I fetched you a pail of water," said Jill.

As Shrek reached for the pail, he was shocked. He looked at his reflection in the water. He was HANDSOME!

"Gorgeous!" said Jill, while the other two maids nodded in agreement.

"Have you ladies seen my donkey?" Shrek asked them.

A beautiful, white steed appeared in the doorway.

"Who are you calling Donkey?" he demanded, "I'm a stallion baby! I can whinny. I can count. That's some quality potion."

Puss read the back of the bottle, "To make the effects of this potion permanent, the drinker must obtain his true love's kiss by midnight," he said.

"Pick me! I'll be your true love," the three maids all insisted, as they tried to kiss Shrek. "Look, ladies, I already have a true love," he told them, backing away.

"Look out, Princess, here comes the new me!" Shrek cut a dashing figure as he rode into town on his noble steed. "Tell Princess Fiona her husband, Sir Shrek, is here to see her," he told a guard at the castle entrance.

Meanwhile, Fiona was washing her face. She saw her reflection in the mirror. She was BEAUTIFUL. Hearing her screams of shock, Shrek rushed into the castle. He spotted a caped figure standing in front of a window.

"Fiona!" he cried. "Hello handsome," said Fairy Godmother.

Hearing Shrek call her name, Fiona ran down the hall. She saw a man silhouetted on the balcony of a nearby room.

"Shrek?!" she gasped in amazement.

"Aye, Fiona, it is me," replied Prince Charming.

"What happened to your voice?" Fiona asked suspiciously.

"The potion changed a lot of things, but not the way I feel about you," Prince Charming told her deceptively.

Across the courtyard Shrek watched as Fiona and Prince Charming embraced. He shouted her name, but she couldn't hear him.

"Don't you think you've already messed her life up enough?" asked Fairy Godmother. "She's finally found the prince of her dreams. It's time you stopped living in a fairy-tale, Shrek. She's a Princess and you're an ogre. That's something no amount of potion is ever going to change."

》》》

Shrek walked sadly down the castle steps to where Donkey and Puss were waiting and they headed for The Poison Apple. "I can't believe you're going to walk away from the best thing that's happened to you," Donkey said, as they downed their drinks. "What choice do I have?" moaned Shrek, "She loves that pretty boy, Prince Charming."

Suddenly the door burst open and the King walked in, but he didn't recognise Shrek and Donkey. He slipped through a door at the back where Fairy Godmother was waiting with Prince Charming. "You'd better have a good reason for dragging us down here," Fairy Godmother told the King. "Yes, you see Fiona isn't really warming up to Prince Charming," the King explained, "I mean you can't force someone to fall in love." "I beg to differ. I do it all the time," said Fairy Godmother, giving the King a potion bottle. "Have Fiona drink this and she'll fall in love with the first man she kisses, which will be Charming" But the King refused. "If you remember, I helped you with your happily ever after and I can take it away just as easily," Fairy Godmother threatened him. "Anyway, we have to go... I need to do Charming's hair before the ball." "Thank you mother," said Charming. "MOTHER?!" exclaimed Donkey. The Fairy Godmother turned to go and spotted Shrek and Donkey. "The Ogre! Stop them! Thieves, bandits!" she shouted.

Back at the swamp, the fairy-tale creatures were watching TV. "Tonight on Knights we've got a white bronco heading into the forest," said the announcer, showing highlights of Shrek, Puss and Donkey's arrest. The fairy-tale creatures didn't realise that the prisoner being dragged away was Shrek, but they recognised his voice shouting, "Find Princess Fiona. Tell her I'm her husband, Shrek." Confused, they stared at the TV, unable to believe their ears.

At the castle, the King prepared two cups of tea. Reluctantly, he uncorked the potion and stirred it into one of the cups. "How about a cup of tea before the ball?" he asked Fiona. "I'm not going," Fiona told him.
"But the whole kingdom's turned out to celebrate your marriage," the King tried to persuade her.
"There's just one problem," Fiona replied, looking down at Prince Charming from her window, "That's not my husband! "
"He is a bit different, but people change for the ones they love. You'd be surprised how much I changed for your mother. Why not give him another chance? You might find you like this new Shrek," the King said guiltily.
"But it's the old one I fell in love with Dad, I'd do anything to have him back."
Fiona reached for her tea, but the king stopped her. "That's mine. Decaf," he said quickly.

⑤ The Story So Far...

Shrek, Donkey and Puss found themselves shackled to the wall in a prison cell.

"I must hold on, before I go totally mad," Puss said to himself.

He looked up to see the fairy-tale creatures peering down at them through a grate. "Too late," he added.

The Three Little Pigs blew the grate off the cell and lowered Pinocchio down. They swung him back and forth but he couldn't quite reach Shrek. Gingy jumped onto Pinocchio's back.

"Tell a lie," said Shrek.

"Something crazy, like I'm wearing ladies' underwear," Donkey suggested.

"I'm wearing ladies' underwear," Pinocchio repeated. Nothing happened.

"Are you?" asked Shrek.

"I most certainly am not," Pinocchio replied, as his nose grew.

Gingy checked Pinocchio's shorts and found a pink thong.

"They're briefs," Pinocchio insisted.

"Are not!" Gingy argued.

"Are too!" Pinocchio replied.

As the argument continued Pinocchio's nose grew longer and longer until Gingy was just inches from Shrek. He unlocked the shackles and Shrek, Donkey and Puss fell to the ground.

"We've gotta stop that kiss! I can't let them do this to Fiona," Shrek declared.

"We'll never get in. The castle is guarded and there's a moat and everything," said Puss.

Then Shrek had an idea. "Do you still know the Muffin Man?" he asked Gingy.
"Sure, hc's down on Drury Lane," Gingy replied.
"We're going to need flour," Shrek told him, "Lots and lots of flour."
So Shrek and Gingy set off to find the Muffin Man.
"Fire up the ovens, Muffin Man, we've got a big order to fill," Gingy said.
Soon the ovens were blazing and the Muffin Man was mixing ingredients in huge vats. Suddenly the house was struck by lightning and strange laughter came from inside.
"It's alive," cried Gingy.

ater that evening in Far Far Away people were screaming and running for cover as a huge shadow loomed over the city. Shrek and Gingy had made a giant gingerbread man and were breaking into the castle!
"Go, baby, go," shouted Gingy.

Meanwhile, inside the castle, Charming waved to the crowd.
"Shrek, what are you doing?" demanded Fiona.
"Just playing the part," Charming replied.
"Is that glitter on your lips?" Fiona asked suspiciously.
"Mmm," said Charming, "Cherry flavoured. Want a taste?"
Fiona turned away in disgust. Seeing Fiona storm off, Fairy Godmother took to the stage.
"Ladies and gentlemen," she announced, "I'd like to dedicate this song to Princess Fiona and Prince Shrek."
The spotlight landed on Fiona and, with all eyes on her, she felt obliged to join Charming on the dance floor.

Back at the castle walls Shrek and Gingy had reached the battlements. "All right big fella, let's crash this party," Shrek yelled.

"Man the catapults!" shouted the captain of the guards as the giant cookie approached the castle. A fireball hit the giant gingerbread man in the chest and set fire to one of his gumdrop buttons.

Enraged he kicked the burning gumdrop over the castle wall. It landed on one of the catapults and smashed it.

"Man the cauldrons!" ordered the Captain. The giant gingerbread man jumped into the moat and grabbed the drawbridge, trying to pull it down. The guards poured an enormous bottle of milk into a massive cauldron and heated it up, then they poured the steaming milk onto the giant cookie. His arms started to dissolve then he groaned and fell backwards into the moat. Shrek leapt through a crack in the drawbridge, slid down the chain and took out the guards at the bottom. Then he lowered the drawbridge and the fairy-tale creatures raced into the castle.

Shrek jumped onto Donkey's back and they headed for the ballroom while Puss fought off the guards who were chasing them. They burst in just as Charming was about to kiss Fiona.

"STOP!!!" yelled Shrek, "Back away from my wife."

"Shrek?" gasped Fiona.

"She's taken the potion, kiss her now!" Fairy Godmother screamed at Charming. Before Fiona could react Charming had planted a huge kiss on her lips.

Fiona stepped towards him, then headbutted him, knocking him unconscious. Fairy Godmother was livid.

"Harold, you were supposed to give her the potion!" she shouted at the King.

"Well, I guess I gave her the wrong tea," he said with a smirk

"Mummy," Charming called out, as he staggered to his feet.

"MUMMY?!" exclaimed Fiona.

The crowd gasped. Fairy Godmother flew up into the air and raised her wand, summoning all her evil powers. As she released her wicked magic, Shrek pushed Fiona to safety, then the King dived in front of Shrek. The King took the full blast, but the magic bounced off his shiny armour straight back to Fairy Godmother, who exploded, leaving just her glasses behind. Fiona and Shrek rushed over to the King. All that remained was his armour.

From inside came a ribbit sound and out jumped a frog.

"Harold?" asked the Queen.

"Dad?" gasped Fiona.

The frog turned to Fiona, "I'd hoped you'd never see me like this," he croaked.

"Man! And he gave you a hard time!" Donkey said to Shrek.

"He's right," the frog agreed. "I'm sorry to both of you. I only wanted what was best for Fiona, but I can see now she already has it. Shrek, Fiona, will you accept an old frog's apologies, and my blessing?"

The Queen scooped up the frog. "I'm sorry, Lillian. I wish I could be the man you deserve," he said. "You're more that man today than you ever were... warts and all," the Queen replied.

Just then the clock chimed midnight. Shrek took Fiona in his arms. "Fiona, is this what you want, to be this way forever? If you kiss me now we can stay like this" he said.
"You'd do that for me," she asked.
"Yes," Shrek said.
Fiona looked at him, then back at her parents.
"I want what any Princess wants... to live happily ever after... with the ogre I married."

As the last chime sounded, Shrek and Fiona kissed and their bodies were transformed back into their ogre selves.

Shrek's Word Search

Can you find all of the ten words hidden in this dastardly difficult Wordsearch? Remember the words can appear forwards, backwards and even diagonally.

P	G	D	L	B	X	X	C	Z	D	B	P
C	I	O	A	Y	N	G	W	R	X	V	U
O	V	N	O	N	T	T	A	C	A	B	S
L	W	K	O	A	O	G	K	E	R	H	S
U	H	E	U	C	O	I	Y	I	U	P	I
D	S	Y	B	N	C	G	F	X	S	W	S
I	O	E	K	R	N	H	S	W	A	M	P
S	Z	J	O	I	G	B	I	V	L	U	L
Q	I	J	G	E	I	T	Y	O	A	D	W
D	E	C	V	C	G	J	E	V	X	G	A
E	H	K	D	L	O	R	A	H	T	R	V
K	J	K	Z	Y	Z	B	Q	I	C	H	R

DONKEY
DRAGON
DULOC

FIONA
GINGY
HAROLD
PINOCCHIO

PUSS
SHREK
SWAMP

Shrek's Crossword

Another challenge awaits! Can you solve this crossword conundrum? From the cryptic clues below, work out all of the answers and complete thepuzzle.

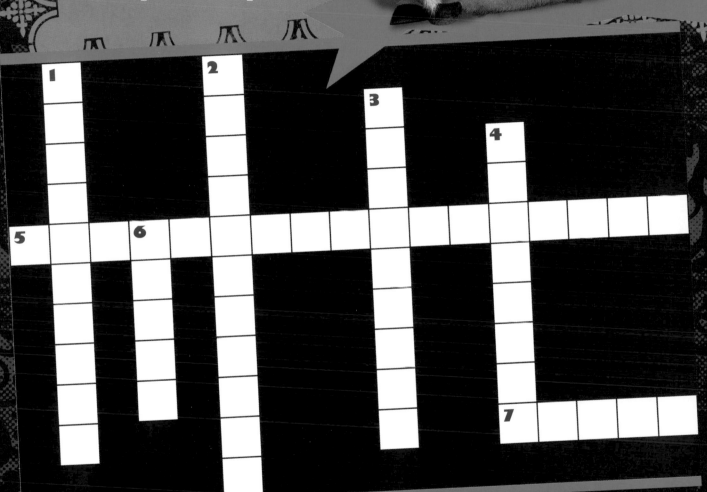

ACROSS

5 She can make all of your dreams come true, for a price

7 A big smelly green ogre

DOWN

1 He locked his daughter in a tower

2 A whiskered assasin

3 If he tells a lie his nose will grow

4 What do you get if you cross a Dragon with a Donkey?

6 If she goes out at night you are in for a fright

Shrek Mega Quiz

How much do you know about Shrek and his friends from Far Far Away. Take this quiz and find out if you are a Shrek MegaFan!

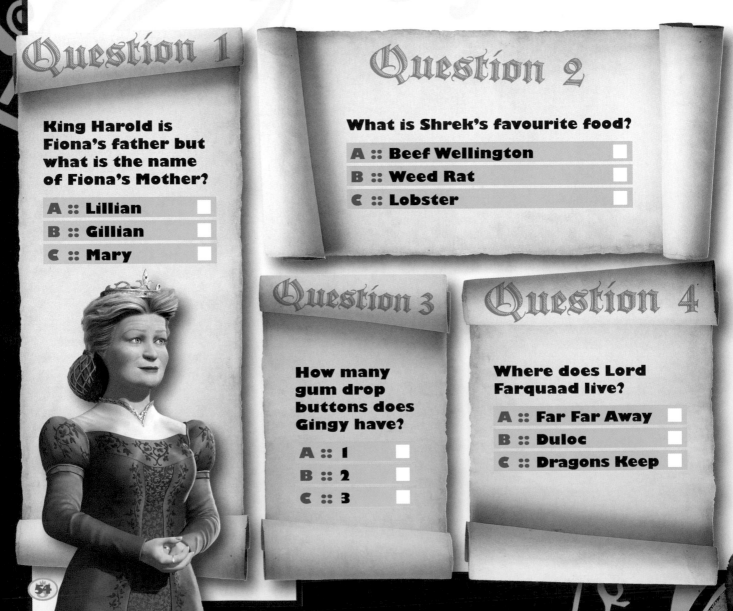

Question 1

King Harold is Fiona's father but what is the name of Fiona's Mother?

A :: Lillian
B :: Gillian
C :: Mary

Question 2

What is Shrek's favourite food?

A :: Beef Wellington
B :: Weed Rat
C :: Lobster

Question 3

How many gum drop buttons does Gingy have?

A :: 1
B :: 2
C :: 3

Question 4

Where does Lord Farquaad live?

A :: Far Far Away
B :: Duloc
C :: Dragons Keep

Question 5

What was the name of the potion Shrek and Donkey drank?

A :: Make yourself handsome ☐

B :: Make yourself grow ☐

C :: Happily Ever After ☐

Question 6

What did Donkey turn into after drinking the potion?

A :: A Dragon ☐

B :: A Frog ☐

C :: A Noble Steed ☐

Question 7

What lie did Pinocchio tell to make his nose grow?

A :: That he wasn't wearingladies underwear ☐

B :: That he was made of gingerbread ☐

C :: That he was a real boy ☐

Question 8

Who made the giant gingerbread man for Shrek?

A :: Gingy ☐

B :: Donkey ☐

C :: The Muffin Man ☐

Question 9

Where do Fiona's parents live?

A :: Quite Far Away ☐

B :: Not That Far Away ☐

C :: Far Far Away ☐

Question 10

How did Shrek and Puss first meet?

A :: Puss was hired to spy on Shrek ☐

B :: Puss was hired to kill Shrek ☐

C :: Puss was hired to clean Shrek's swamp ☐

Ginger Pairs

The are six Gingerbread Men sets of twins on these ages. Can you find the matching pairs? Be careful though, some of the differences are very small.

Answers

A = ☐ B = ☐ C = ☐ D = ☐ E = ☐ F = ☐

57

Follow The Fly

Join up the flies to reveal a picture of Puss and Donkey!

Dinner Time Hide and Seek

Can you find all eight of these items hidden around King Harold's dinner table? Look really closely as some of them are really well hidden.

Merlin is the Worcestershire Academy's former magic teacher. He's an eccentric recluse who has retired to the tranquility of nature to discover his divine purpose. All he wants to do is be left alone in peace. His magic is rusty, and his techniques are extreme, but ultimately he proves to be a helpful resource for Shrek and the boys.

Merlin

Arthur Pendragon is Fiona's cousin and the next heir to the throne. He is your average scrawny teenager. When Shrek informs him that he needs to take over the ruling of Far Far Away, Arthur is thrilled to leave school and become king!

Artie

SHREK THE THIRD™

When the ogre Shrek married Princess Fiona, becoming the next King and Queen of Far Far Away wasn't part of the plan. So when his father-in-law, King Harold, falls ill, it is up to Shrek to find a suitable heir or he will be forced to give up his beloved swamp for the throne – a dream to a prince, but a nightmare to any self-respecting ogre. Compounding the pressure, Shrek has just learned that he and Fiona are soon to be the parents of a bouncing baby ogre.

Recruiting his friends Donkey and Puss in Boots for a new quest, Shrek sets out to bring back the rightful heir to the throne — Fiona's cousin Artie. They soon discover that the only thing the rebellious teenager is good at is working Shrek's last nerve…and this preview of parenthood isn't doing much for the ogre's confidence as a father-to-be.

Back in Far Far Away, Fiona's jilted Prince Charming seizes his chance to claim the throne, storming the city with an army of fairy tale villains. But they have a surprise in store, because Fiona, together with her mother, Queen Lillian, has drafted her fellow fairy tale heroines to defend their "happily ever afters."

As Shrek, Donkey and Puss work on changing Artie from a royal pain in the you-know-what into a once and future king, Fiona and her band of princesses must stop Prince Charming and ensure there will be a kingdom left to rule.

Check out some more of the new faces you can expect to see in Shrek The Third!

Shrek and

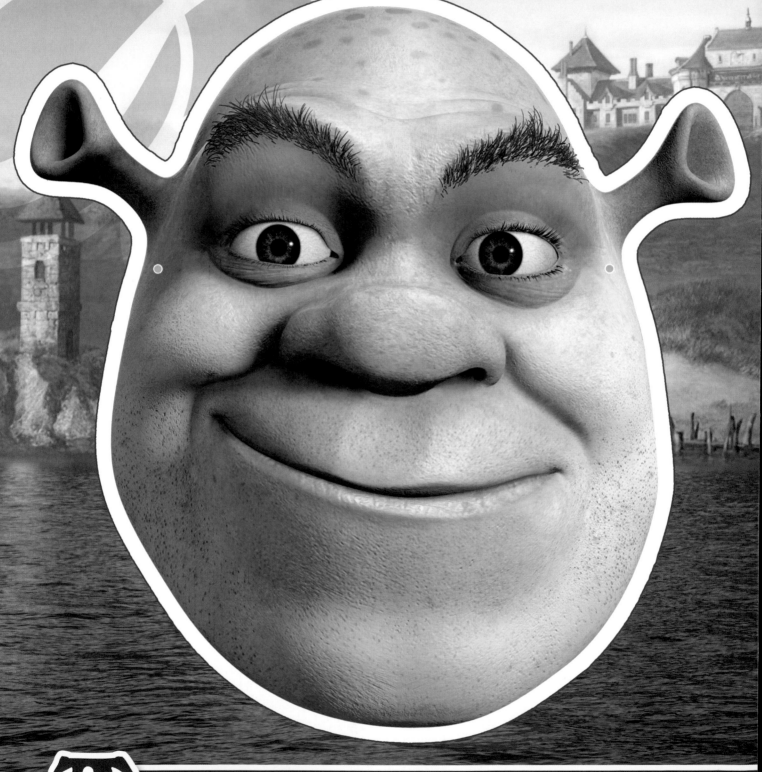

Fiona Mask

some elastic through the holes. Now you are ready to scare any
unsuspecting subjects who happen to knock on your castle door!

Answers

P31 Spot The Difference

P52 Shrek's Word Search

P	G	D	L	B	X	X	C	Z	D	B	P
C	I	O	A	Y	N	G	W	R	X	V	U
O	V	N	O	N	T	T	A	C	A	B	S
L	W	K	O	A	O	G	K	E	R	H	S
U	H	E	U	C	O	I	Y	I	U	P	I
D	S	Y	B	N	C	G	F	X	S	W	S
I	O	E	K	R	N	H	S	W	A	M	P
S	Z	J	O	I	G	B	I	V	L	U	L
Q	I	J	G	E	I	T	Y	O	A	D	W
D	E	C	V	C	G	J	E	V	X	G	A
E	H	K	D	L	O	R	A	H	T	R	V
K	J	K	Z	Y	Z	B	Q	I	C	H	R

P54 Shrek Mega Quiz

1.A • 2.B • 3.B • 4.B • 5.C • 6.C
7.A • 8.C • 9.C • 10.B

P53 Shrek's Crossword

KING
PUSSINBOOTS
PINOCCHIO
DRONKEYS
THEFAIRYGODMOTHER
HAROLD
FIONA
SHREK

P57 Ginger Pairs

A.6 • B.1 • C.5 • D.4 • E.2 • F.3

68